THREE TRIO SONATAS FOR FLUTE OR VIOLIN

VIVALDI
Sonata in C Minor, RV83

BOISMORTIER
Sonata in E Minor

TELEMANN
Sonata in B-Flat Major

PLAYBACK+
Speed • Pitch • Balance • Loop

To access audio visit:
www.halleonard.com/mylibrary

Enter Code
4610-0173-5142-5073

ISBN 978-1-59615-688-3

© 2005 MMO Music Group, Inc.
All Rights Reserved

Visit Hal Leonard Online at
www.halleonard.com

Contact us:
Hal Leonard
7777 West Bluemound Road
Milwaukee, WI 53213
Email: info@halleonard.com

In Europe, contact:
Hal Leonard Europe Limited
42 Wigmore Street
Marylebone, London, W1U 2RN
Email: info@halleonardeurope.com

In Australia, contact:
Hal Leonard Australia Pty. Ltd.
4 Lentara Court
Cheltenham, Victoria, 3192 Australia
Email: info@halleonard.com.au

THREE TRIO SONATAS
FOR
FLUTE OR VIOLIN

VIVALDI
Sonata in C Minor, RV83

BOISMORTIER
Sonata in E Minor

TELEMANN
Sonata in B-Flat Major

CONTENTS

VIVALDI

Sonata in C minor for Violin (Flute), Cello and Piano.

4 taps (1 measure)
precede music.

Allegro (molto moderato ♩ = 80)

4 taps (1 measure) precede music.
Start on upbeat of 4th tap.

BOISMORTIER
Sonata in E minor for Violin (Flute), Viola da Gamba and Basso continuo.

4 taps (1 measure)
precede music.

2

Adagio

2 taps precede pickup on
upbeat of 2nd tap

3

Allegro

8

TELEMANN

Sonata in Bb major for Violin (Flutè), Solo Cembalo (Piano and Basso continuo).

Siciliana ♪ = 108   6 taps (1/2 measure)
precede music.

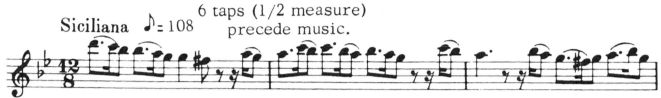